I'm Thankful Each Day!

P.K. Hallinan

CHILDRENS PRESS, CHICAGO

School & Library Edition

Copyright © MCMLXXXI by Patrick Hallinan
Milwaukee, Wisconsin 53201
All rights reserved. Printed and bound in U.S.A.
Published simultaneously in Canada.

New ISBN 0-516-09180-8
Former ISBN 0-8249-8008-5

I'm thankful each day
for the blessings I see
and for all of the gifts
that are given to me.

And counting the stars
at the edge of the sea,

I can't help but feel
they were put there for me.

I'm thankful for summers
and warm golden days...

I'm thankful for autumns of orange pumpkin haze.

I'm thankful for meadows
and bright colored flowers...

I'm thankful for raindrops
and soft summer showers.

Each sunset is special ...

Each sunrise is new...

Each breeze in the tree
is a promise come true

Each evening's a wonder
where beauty abounds…

Each morning's a harvest
of new sights and sounds.

And it's nice just to know
that beneath winter snow
the blossoms of spring
are beginning to grow.

I'm thankful for friends
for laughing and sharing...

I'm thankful for family
for loving and caring.

I'm thankful for all
the kindness I see...

I'm thankful for peace
and for pure harmony.

My body's a present
of perfect design...

My mind is a power
as endless as time.

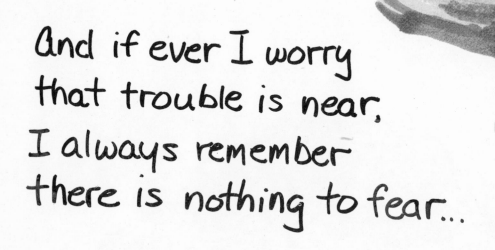

And if ever I worry
that trouble is near,
I always remember
there is nothing to fear...

For each hour is laden
with infinite love ...

Each second brings comfort and joy from above.

And I guess in the end
the best thing to say
is I'm thankful for living...

I'm thankful each day!